The Balanced Mind

The Balanced Mind

A Mental Health Journal
Creative Prompts and Effective Practices

Carolyn Mehlomakulu, LMFT-S, ATR-BC

ROCKRIDGE
PRESS

Interior and Cover Designer: Michael Cook
Art Producer: Megan Baggott
Editor: Carolyn Abate
Production Editor: Mia Moran
Cover Illustration: Liana Monica Bordei/iStock
Author photo courtesy of Christine St. Laurent

ISBN: Print 978-1-64611-767-3
R0

Introduction

Anxiety has always been a part of my life, even before I knew to label it as such. I've also struggled with depression at times. This hasn't been a big concern for me in many years, but I still watch for signs of my mood getting out of balance so I can be proactive in addressing it.

As an art therapist and psychotherapist, I have learned many tools and strategies that support both my own mental health and that of my clients. When things seem to be getting off track or I notice that negative emotions are rising up more often than not, I remind myself to use the tools that help me through it all: listening to my emotions, exploring what is going on in my life or internal world that needs to be addressed, and then taking helpful action.

Creativity and art have been important parts of my own self-care in order to live a fulfilling life. Since childhood, making art has been a source of relaxation, joy, play, self-expression, and pride. My early love of art and crafts led to my interest in pursuing art therapy as a career. Now I enjoy being able to use art therapy to guide others through their own journey of understanding themselves, learning to cope with emotions and challenges in life, accessing their inner strengths, and healing from past experiences.

Journaling—in written and art form—provides a means to express your thoughts and feelings. This method of expression can provide a helpful release to get things out of your head and onto the page. This journal will take things even further. The guided writing prompts will help you look at things from a new perspective, practice new mind-sets, be more mindful of positive aspects of your life, and identify helpful steps you can take. The creative prompts give you another way to explore and express your thoughts and feelings, as well as a tool for mindfulness and relaxation. Art-making has been shown to have a positive impact on mental health, leading to decreased stress levels, increased positive mood, and a sense of mastery.

My hope is that through these written and creative exercises you will feel more present and grounded as you are able to gain more self-awareness, learn new ways to see things in your life, take action in a way that supports your mental health, improve your mood, and access the soothing and healing benefits of creativity.

Your Mental Health

Mental health refers to your psychological, emotional, and social well-being. Good mental health does not mean that you feel happy all the time: It's when you're in touch with and aware of your own thoughts and feelings. You can cope with everyday stress and difficult life events, all while living a fulfilling and meaningful life. Although everyone feels uncomfortable emotions at times or goes through moments of stress, good mental health means being able to move through that distress with self-care, hope, and connection to others.

Everyone should be aware of the need to take care of their mental health, just as they take care of their physical health. However, some people experience more mental health concerns than others. Whatever impacts your own mental health—biology, stresses of daily life, traumatic and difficult life experiences, or poor relationships with others—you can help improve your own mental health through positive coping and support from others.

Good mental health is an ongoing process, not a one-time goal that you reach and take for granted. There may be ups and downs as you experience different stresses or forget to put your tools into action, but you can always recommit to working on your own mental health. As you spend more time understanding who you are, expressing yourself, practicing self-care, and connecting in meaningful relationships, your mental health will continue to improve and strengthen.

In this journal, we will explore four pillars of mental health:

- **Learn to regulate your emotions and reactions.** This includes understanding your feelings and thoughts, identifying triggers, and accepting emotions without dwelling in negativity or

letting them control you. It's also about creating a more balanced mind-set, challenging unhelpful thinking, and learning
strategies that increase positive emotions in your life.

- **Practice mindfulness.** Mindfulness means being aware of
  the present moment or a singular focus while having a nonjudgmental attitude. Many people think only of meditation
  when they think of mindfulness, but there are many ways
  to practice being mindful throughout your day. Mindfulness
  helps you become more aware of your thoughts and feelings,
  respond to stressors intentionally rather than reactively, and
  feel more grounded and calm.

- **Make movement a priority.** Movement and exercise are great
  ways to release stress and improve mental health. There
  are many ways to incorporate more movement into your
  life, so it's important to figure out what works for you and
  what you most enjoy. This can include vigorous exercise that
  helps relieve stress, calming movement that helps you feel
  grounded and relaxed, playful activities that bring fun into
  your life, and even daily activities and chores.

- **Build lasting relationships and meaningful connections.**
  Healthy, meaningful relationships are essential to good
  mental health. This includes being your authentic self in
  relationships, reciprocal care and affection, strength through
  the support of others, a sense of belonging, and healthy
  boundaries.

How to Use This Journal

This journal includes a variety of prompts to help you build awareness of your thoughts and feelings, implement new coping skills, and make positive changes in your life. The writing prompts will either give you a topic to reflect on through journaling or ask you to try an activity and write about your experience. The creative prompts will guide you through art activities that promote positive emotion and relaxation, help you practice mindfulness, or encourage self-reflection. There are check-in prompts interspersed throughout to help with self-assessment.

There are a few things you may want to keep in mind as you use this journal:

- It is best to work through the journal in the order that it is laid out, as some skills and reflection questions build on each other. In addition, related topics are often grouped together to help you explore various aspects of a concept through both writing and art. However, if you come to a particular prompt that you don't feel ready to complete at the moment, move on and then come back later.

- Let go of any pressure or expectations for yourself with the creative prompts. You do not need to be good at art to use creativity for stress reduction and self-exploration. As you work on the creative prompts, remind yourself that whatever you do is good enough. Focus on the process and try to have some fun with it.

- Most of the creative activities let you choose the art media to use. You don't need to buy a bunch of supplies, but this may be a good opportunity to try something new. At a minimum, you will need a basic pencil or pen and something for color. For any drawing and painting media, you might want to consider using colored pencils, markers, oil or chalk pastels, and watercolor paint. If you want to try collage, you will need scissors, a glue stick, and magazines to cut out images.

- Please remember that although this journal is designed to support your mental health and self-reflection, it is not a replacement for therapy. If you have significant depression, anxiety, or trauma, you may benefit from seeking additional professional help.

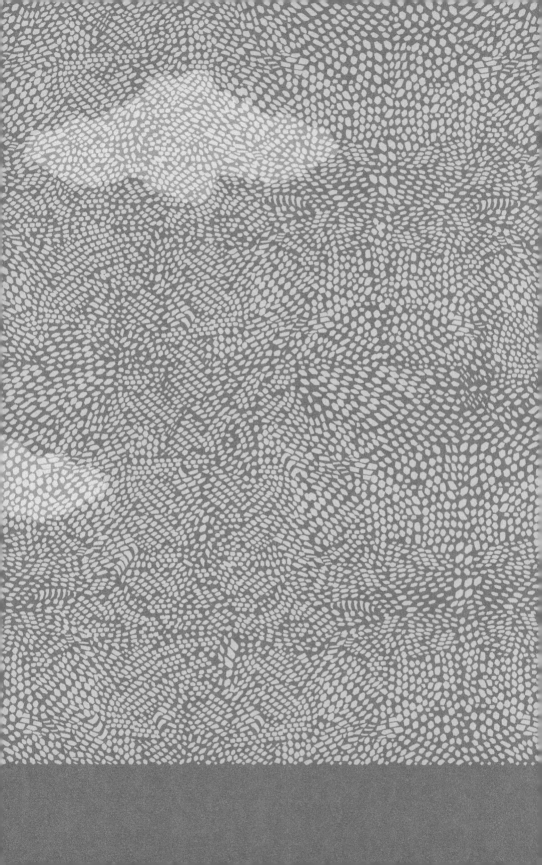

"Your vision will become clear only when you can look into your own heart. . . . Who looks outside, dreams; who looks inside, awakes."

CARL JUNG

How would you describe your mental health currently?
What emotions are you hoping to increase or decrease in your life? What are some of the things that are currently causing you stress in your life and impacting your mental health? What would "better" look like for you? Write down the top three things that you hope to change.

_____

_____

_____

_____

_____

_____

_____

_____

_____

_____

_____

_____

_____

_____

_____

_____

Think about an emotion that you would like to experience more of in your life, and then draw or paint it on this page. As a reminder, you don't have to consider yourself an artist to express yourself creatively. What colors do you associate with this feeling? What does it look like? Your image could be abstract—just colors, lines, and shapes that don't look like anything specific. It could be a symbol, image, or pattern that comes to mind. As you work, notice if you are able to experience that feeling at all by focusing on it during the art process.

"Only be attentive to that which rises up in you and set it above everything that you observe about you. What goes on in your innermost self is worthy of your whole love; you must somehow keep working at it."

RAINER MARIA RILKE

Becoming aware of and accepting emotions are the first steps in being able to manage them. The act of identifying and naming your emotional state, out loud or on paper, can help lower the intensity of that feeling. Take some time to write about how you are feeling; can you identify and name at least three emotions that you felt today? Write about the situations that led to those feelings. (Turn to page 154 for a list of emotion words, if you need help.)

_____

_____

_____

_____

_____

_____

_____

_____

_____

_____

_____

"Don't believe everything you think. Thoughts are just that—thoughts."

ALLAN LOKOS

People often believe that an event or situation is the trigger for their negative feelings. On the contrary, it's their thoughts or interpretations that actually impact their mood. Write about a recent upsetting situation, such as a relationship conflict, a work problem, or something that didn't go as you wanted.

How did you feel? What thoughts came up for you during that experience? Take a moment to examine if they're actually true. What evidence supports these thoughts, and what evidence makes them not true? How can you rewrite these thoughts so that they are more balanced and less upsetting?

_____

_____

_____

_____

_____

_____

_____

_____

_____

Check-in: Now that you have completed a few prompts, take some time to reflect. What has it been like for you to work on being more aware of and expressive of your thoughts and feelings? Write about a situation recently in which you were aware of your emotions. What helpful actions or self-talk did you use to manage your emotions?

_____

_____

_____

_____

_____

_____

_____

_____

_____

_____

_____

_____

_____

_____

A body scan is a mindfulness tool that can help you be more aware of physical sensations and emotions and feel grounded. It helps get you in the practice of observing how your body reacts to experiences. So, close your eyes. Focus your attention on each part of your body, starting at your feet and working your way up to your head. Draw the outline of a body and then add colors, lines, and symbols to represent what you noticed during your body scan.

Once you have identified your emotions, it can be helpful to further explore what these emotions are telling you. Unpleasant feelings often signal an unmet need. Write down at least three emotions you have felt today. For the negative emotions, what do you need in order to feel better? For the positive emotions, what fulfilled needs do these point to? Think about how you can take action to address the unmet needs and increase the positive moments. Write down your ideas.

"Negative emotions like loneliness, envy, and guilt have an important role to play in a happy life; they're big, flashing signs that something needs to change."

GRETCHEN RUBIN

Becoming more aware of your thoughts and self-talk can help you understand and manage your emotions. What's a current worry that caused you to feel upset? Write about all the thoughts, memories, and self-talk that came up for you in the situation. Then review what you wrote and try to identify which thoughts may be either unhelpful or untrue. Rewrite those thoughts in a more balanced way.

"Change your thoughts and you can change your world."

NORMAN VINCENT PEALE

It can be helpful to remember that your feelings are always changing, just like the weather. When you notice a negative mood or intense emotional reaction to something, remember that you will not be stuck in it forever, but you may want to do something to cope with it until it passes. Take a few minutes to check in with yourself and notice your own emotional weather for today. Draw or paint an image of weather and a landscape that represents your current feelings and mood.

Unhealthy coping strategies can create new problems or make you feel worse. Recognizing the unhelpful strategies that you tend to fall back on is important. It can help you focus on new, healthy coping techniques that lead to improved mental health and a more fulfilling life.

Unhealthy coping may include drinking too much, isolating yourself, emotional eating, or spending too much time online. List some of the unhealthy ways that you cope or distract yourself when you're upset. What are some of the negative consequences of your unhealthy coping?

_____

_____

_____

_____

_____

_____

_____

_____

_____

_____

_____

"My mission in life is not merely to survive, but to thrive; and to do so with some passion, some compassion, some humor, and some style."

MAYA ANGELOU

You always have the capacity for change and progress.
What is a change that you want to make in your life and
what is your motivation? Do you want to start a new healthy
habit, change careers, spend more quality time with family,
or something else?

Identify some of the possible obstacles or beliefs that get in
the way of this change. Write down the internal and external
resources that you will draw on to make this change and
then create an action plan of your steps.

_____

_____

_____

_____

_____

_____

_____

_____

_____

_____

_____

_____

"What would it be like if you lived each day, each breath, as a work of art in progress? Imagine that you are a masterpiece unfolding, every second of every day. . . . A work of art taking form with each breath."

THOMAS CRUM

What is something that symbolizes hope for you? It could be something that you see in nature, a goal for the future, or even an abstract symbol. Draw or paint your symbol of hope. Remember that your personal meaning and self-expression in the art are more important than how good your art looks.

Check-in: It's time for another check-in. Although it can be easy to focus only on what is going wrong, remember to pay attention to exceptions—moments of positive emotions or things that are going well. Write down some recent examples of times that you felt good. What helped make these moments better?

_____

_____

_____

_____

_____

_____

_____

_____

_____

_____

_____

_____

_____

It can be helpful to try to respond to your own emotions with nonjudgment. This means not immediately pushing them aside or assuming they're bad. What is an emotion that you tend to invalidate in yourself or struggle to accept and express? What beliefs come up around this feeling? What about the people, experiences, and messages that have shaped your judgment? Write down a new, validating statement that you will tell yourself the next time this emotion comes up.

"Our feelings are not there to be cast out or conquered. They're there to be engaged and expressed with imagination and intelligence."

T. K. COLEMAN

Practicing mindful breathing can help you build awareness and shift your emotions. First, jot down your current mood and stress level. Then sit in silence for a few minutes and try to focus on just your breathing. When your mind wanders (which is expected and normal), notice those thoughts and then bring your attention back to your breath. Write down how you feel after the mindfulness break. What was this experience like for you and what were some of the thoughts that came up? What level is your stress at now?

"Learn to get in touch with the silence within yourself and know that everything in this life has a purpose."

ELISABETH KÜBLER-ROSS

Drawing your breath can help you mindfully connect with your body and your breathing. Choose any drawing material (I like oil pastels for this, but pencils or markers work well too). Bring your attention to the feeling of your breath. Begin to draw by moving your hand to the rhythm of your breathing. This could be a line that goes up with each inhale and down with each exhale, a series of circles, or just a line that meanders around the page. Do what feels right. Next, slow your breathing so that you are taking deep, relaxing breaths while you continue to draw. You can leave your final drawing as is or go back to develop an image by adding designs.

The 5-4-3-2-1 grounding technique helps you turn away from anxious or distressing thoughts and feel more calm. It works by connecting you with your body and helping you notice the world around you so that you feel more grounded in the present. Sit quietly and notice—without judgment—five things you can see, four things you can feel, three things you can hear, two things you can smell, and one thing you can taste. Write down what came to mind and how the practice impacted your anxiety or stress level.

_____

_____

_____

_____

_____

_____

_____

_____

_____

_____

_____

"The best way to capture moments is to pay attention. This is how we cultivate mindfulness."

JON KABAT-ZINN

Everyone has the capacity to create, even if you don't see yourself as particularly artistic. Creative activity can help lower stress and bring a sense of fulfillment. Creative thinking can help you see things in a new way. What are ways that you are creative?

Beyond art-making, creativity can include gardening, decorating your home, editing photos, cooking, playing music, writing, crafting, and even creative problem-solving or coming up with new ideas. What is something you could do to bring more creativity to your life? Do you have any beliefs or self-talk about creativity that you need to challenge and rewrite?

_____

_____

_____

_____

_____

_____

_____

_____

_____

_____

"There's no such thing as creative people and non-creative people. There are only people who use their creativity and people who don't. Unused creativity doesn't just disappear. It lives within us until it's expressed, neglected to death, or suffocated by resentment and fear."

BRENÉ BROWN

Mindful, focused doodling can be a relaxing activity. Begin by dividing the page into several smaller sections, creating approximately 8 to 15 different areas. Try scribbling or tracing something several times across the page, or simply draw lines. Use a pen, fine-tip marker, or pencil to fill each section with a pattern.

Remember to keep your focus on your drawing. Bring your attention back to the page if you notice that your mind wanders. If your doodle is very detailed, this page may take a long time to complete, so feel free to work on it over several sessions. How do you feel after working on your doodle?

Check-in: How have your mood and stress levels been lately? Identify some of the factors—both positive and negative—that have impacted how you are feeling. What has been the most helpful practice in addressing your mental health? Is there one thing that you can commit to doing more of to help yourself?

"Caring for your body, mind, and spirit is your greatest and grandest responsibility. It's about listening to the needs of your soul and then honoring them."

KRISTI LING

When you think about self-care, what comes to mind?
What are some of your own beliefs about self-care? Do messages from others or your own self-talk get in the way? Write down some of the activities that are essential to your own self-care and commit to making more time for them. (Turn to page 156 for a list of self-care ideas.)

Create a self-care collage. Using your personal self-care list (from page 38) as inspiration, fill this pages with images that represent your self-care activities. (You can also turn to page 156 for other self-care ideas.) To create your collage, you can cut out images from magazines to glue into your journal, draw a collection of symbols, or do a combination of both. Notice what emotions come up as you work and when you look at your finished collage.

Practicing self-compassion starts with recognizing that it's normal for you to make mistakes and struggle, while still giving yourself the same compassion and gentleness that you would show to a close friend or loved one when they're in need. Turning self-judgment into self-compassion can soothe your emotions during a difficult time and motivate you to keep moving forward.

Think of a situation that triggers a feeling of failure. Write about that situation and some of the self-critical thoughts that come up. Think about how you could talk to yourself in that situation from a place of self-compassion instead and write down your ideas.

_____

_____

_____

_____

_____

_____

_____

_____

_____

_____

_____

*"When we give
ourselves compassion,
we are opening our hearts in a way
that can transform our lives."*

KRISTIN NEFF

What is something that you need to let go of? Maybe it is a regret, a past hurt, a belief that no longer serves you, or an unrealized dream. Write about the situation that you are still holding on to. How would it feel to let go and move on? End your writing session with a helpful statement that you want to remember in the process of letting go.

"Some people believe holding on and hanging in there are signs of great strength. However, there are times when it takes much more strength to know when to let go and then do it."

ANN LANDERS

Art can help you express your emotions and see them in a different way. Think about a stressful emotion that you are struggling with, such as anxiety, depression, or anger. Create an abstract image that expresses that feeling. Choose colors that you associate with the feeling, and then use lines and shapes to express it on the page.

Remember that the art you create here is about expression; try not to focus on the aesthetics. After completing your image, write a supportive statement to yourself about this feeling using your tools: self-validation, nonjudgment, and recognizing needs.

What is your current level of movement and exercise?
How do you feel about that? Identify and write down some of the barriers and mental blocks that get in the way of prioritizing movement for you. Think about internal factors (such as doubts and fears) and external factors (such as the weather and your location).

Brainstorm some coping strategies that you can use to overcome these obstacles. Decide on a new intention or belief that you want to remember when it comes to movement and exercise, and then write it down. Now set one small goal for increased movement during the next week.

_____

_____

_____

_____

_____

_____

_____

_____

_____

_____

"The first step towards getting somewhere is to decide that you are not going to stay where you are."

J. P. MORGAN

Instead of thinking of movement as an obligation or chore, try to reconnect with the joy and fun of such an experience. Think of a positive memory related to movement—running around with friends as a child, a challenging but beautiful hike, playing on a sports team, or a peaceful moment in yoga.

Write about that memory and the feelings associated with it. Then brainstorm a list of movement activities you would like to try or do more of. Think about a mix of options—movement that is fun, movement that helps you feel peaceful and content, and vigorous movement that helps release stress.

_____

_____

_____

_____

_____

_____

_____

_____

_____

*"When you do things from your soul,
you feel a river moving in you, a joy."*

RUMI

Notice the impact that movement has on your mood.
Before you do a movement activity, journal about your current stressor, mood, and energy level. Now pick an activity that you enjoy—going for a walk or run, practicing yoga, playing a sport with a friend—and get moving.

Come back to this page afterward to write about the experience. What is your mood and energy level after your movement activity? Do you have any new ideas or thoughts to help you address your current stresses? Can you write down more helpful thoughts about the impact of movement that you want to remember in the future?

_____

_____

_____

_____

_____

_____

_____

_____

_____

_____

_____

"If you are in a bad mood go for a walk. If you are still in a bad mood go for another walk."

HIPPOCRATES

Check-in: It's important to notice and celebrate all of the progress that you make, even small steps in the right direction. What is an example of your recent progress or a change that you have been able to make? How does it feel to acknowledge and honor this progress?

_____

_____

_____

_____

_____

_____

_____

_____

_____

_____

_____

_____

_____

Energy drawings can build self-awareness by connecting you with your own emotions, energy, and body. To create an energy drawing, first spend a few minutes with your eyes closed, observing your breathing, how your body feels, your energy level, and your current emotions. When you feel ready, put lines, shapes, and colors on the page to represent your energy and emotions. Try not to overthink this. Simply move your hand in a way that feels right to you and expresses your current state. As you work, you might also add colors or lines that represent your capacity to draw energy from your own inner strength or something greater outside of you.

Practicing gratitude can help you appreciate what you have in your life instead of focusing on what you wish was different. Think of at least 10 things that you are grateful for today, both big and small, and write about them.

_____

_____

_____

_____

_____

_____

_____

_____

_____

_____

_____

_____

_____

_____

_____

"The little things?
The little moments?
They aren't little."

JON KABAT-ZINN

Developing a soothing routine can help you better manage upsetting emotions and the stress of life. To begin, go through each of your senses—sight, smell, taste, touch, and sound—and write down at least three soothing things in each category. Now, write down what you find to be comforting from other people when you are upset. You can make an effort to include these things in your daily life, as well as turn to them when you are feeling anxious or sad.

_____

_____

_____

_____

_____

_____

_____

_____

_____

_____

_____

_____

_____

"Do something every day that is loving toward your body and gives you the opportunity to enjoy the sensations of your body."

GOLDA PORETSKY

Put on some music that feels joyful or calming to you, preferably something without lyrics. Take a moment to close your eyes and listen. When you're ready, open your eyes and begin to draw or paint in response to the music, moving your hand to the rhythm. Consider creating something abstract, simply using lines, shapes, and colors that reflect the song. Stay mindful as you work, keeping your awareness on the music, the movement of your body, and your drawing.

Sometimes it can help to step back and notice what we do have control over. Think about a situation that is currently challenging, such as a problem at work or a difficult relationship. What are the things that you can't control in this situation? What are the things that you can control? How can you focus more of your energy on what you can control in order to improve the situation? What are some next steps you want to take?

_____

_____

_____

_____

_____

_____

_____

_____

_____

_____

_____

_____

"Your present circumstances don't determine where you can go; they merely determine where you start."

NIDO QUBEIN

Check-in: Even as you make progress with your mental health, there will be difficult times. What has been challenging lately? Write a note of self-compassion to yourself; remind yourself that struggling sometimes is normal, encourage yourself kindly to keep working on things, and celebrate the moments that you managed things well.

_____

_____

_____

_____

_____

_____

_____

_____

_____

_____

_____

_____

_____

_____

Get out in nature! Explore your neighborhood park, hike in the woods, or simply sit in your own backyard. Practice being mindfully present by looking for things that interest you or moments of beauty. If you are able, bring your journal with you and draw what you notice. If you are able, bring your journal with you and draw what you notice. Remember that you do not need to be good at art; just focus on having fun.

Take some time to assess the relationships in your life—
family, friends, and coworkers or classmates. What are the
most important things for you to have in your relationships?
Who are the people who currently support you? Are there
any unhealthy relationships that you need to separate from?
Is there anything you want to change about the amount of
time you spend with others, your social activities, the level
of connection, or how your relationships make you feel?

"The things that matter most in our lives are not fantastic or grand. They are moments when we touch one another."

JACK KORNFIELD

"Daring to set boundaries is about having the courage to love ourselves even when we risk disappointing others."

BRENÉ BROWN

Having good boundaries is an essential part of healthy, fulfilling relationships. They allow you to speak up for your own needs, set limits to protect yourself from hurt and resentment, and build mutual trust in relationships. Being able to say no to others is one aspect of setting good boundaries.

Think about a relationship, in which you'd like to be able to say no and set firmer boundaries. Write about the relationship as well as the fears and beliefs that make it hard for you to hold boundaries. What are two or three things you can commit to doing differently in these relationships?

_____

_____

_____

_____

_____

_____

_____

_____

_____

_____

_____

Vulnerability and openness lead to more meaningful connections with others. What are some of the barriers you face in being vulnerable and trusting in relationships? What relationships would you like to be more open in? What would it look like? Would sharing something important about your feelings be helpful? Remember that you should not trust everyone or be fully open in every situation, so choose a safe person to be more open with.

_____

_____

_____

_____

_____

_____

_____

_____

_____

_____

_____

_____

"We're never so vulnerable than when we trust someone—but paradoxically, if we cannot trust, neither can we find love or joy."

WALTER ANDERSON

Use symbols and color to represent your current relation-
ships and boundaries. Draw one symbol or shape that
represents you and, then others that represent some of the
people in your life. You can use different colors to show
emotions related to those people and add lines to represent
boundaries and connections, altering the thickness of the
lines to represent the strength of that boundary or connection. After looking at your completed image, make changes
to reflect more healthy relationships and boundaries.

Check-in: Sometimes change feels uncomfortable. Even when you want things to be different, you might still feel uncomfortable when you try to handle things in a new way. What have been some new actions that have been uncomfortable for you to try? What motivates you to push through this discomfort?

_____

_____

_____

_____

_____

_____

_____

_____

_____

_____

_____

_____

_____

"To be passive is to let others decide for you. To be aggressive is to decide for others. To be assertive is to decide for yourself. And to trust that there is enough, that you are enough."

EDITH EVA EGER

Assertiveness means being able to clearly communicate your thoughts, feelings, and needs without trying to hurt anyone else. You don't suppress your feelings or avoid conflict, but you also don't lash out at others. What is a way that you want to practice being more assertive and honest in your relationships? For some people this might include expressing how you feel more often or speaking up when you disagree with something. What beliefs or messages from others have gotten in the way of this in the past?

_____

_____

_____

_____

_____

_____

_____

_____

_____

_____

_____

Write about a relationship, past or present, that is difficult for you or that you want to repair. This doesn't have to be a romantic relationship; it can be with your boss, a family member, or a former friend.

Why is improving this relationship important to you? Shift your perspective by writing about how the other person might view you and the relationship. Now, focus on what strengths and values they have, and what good they have brought to your life. What is one thing you have learned from this reflection to hold on to as you move forward?

_____

_____

_____

_____

_____

_____

_____

_____

_____

_____

_____

"Things don't change. You change your way of looking, that's all."

CARLOS CASTANEDA

Visualization can help you contain or let go of upsetting memories and intense emotions. Close your eyes for a moment and visualize an image that represents protection from something or the act of letting go. Draw or paint that image here. When distressing feelings or memories come up later, call that image to mind to help manage the feeling. Some ideas include leaves floating past on a stream, clouds blowing through the sky, a balloon floating away, or a protective wall.

Think about a relationship, past or present, that has taught you something important about love and connection. Write about that person and the relationship. Is there something from the experience of that relationship that you need to remember or apply in your life now?

_____

_____

_____

_____

_____

_____

_____

_____

_____

_____

_____

_____

_____

_____

"The most important thing in life is to learn how to give out love, and to let it come in."

MITCH ALBOM

One way to help yourself feel better is to do something kind for someone else. Engage in acts of kindness and generosity for loved ones, friends, or even strangers. As you do some of these activities, notice how you feel and then come back to this page to write about the experiences and how they impacted your mood.

_____

_____

_____

_____

_____

_____

_____

_____

_____

_____

_____

_____

_____

"Love and kindness are never wasted.
They always make a difference.
They bless the one who receives
them, and they bless you, the giver."

BARBARA DE ANGELIS

Practicing mindfulness in your relationships means being truly present when communicating with the other person. That means setting aside judgments, preconceptions, or distractions. What are some of the things that get in the way of you truly listening to someone when they talk, especially when it is a difficult conversation?

Make some notes. Are you busy rehearsing your own response, becoming defensive, or daydreaming about something else? The next time you talk, try to practice active listening and being mindfully present in that conversation and, then come back to this page and write about the experience.

_____

_____

_____

_____

_____

_____

_____

_____

_____

"It takes two to speak the truth—
one to speak, and another to hear."

HENRY DAVID THOREAU

Check-in: As you have worked through this journal, what changes have you noticed in your relationships? Identify a recent time when you have felt a strong sense of connection with others. What have you done recently to build or strengthen fulfilling relationships in your life?

_____

_____

_____

_____

_____

_____

_____

_____

_____

_____

_____

_____

_____

_____

The mind often focuses on worries, stresses, and expectations about the future, or dwells on past events and regrets. Try to check in with yourself throughout the day tomorrow and ask if you are focusing on the present moment or something else. Come back to this page to write about what you noticed. How often are you living in either the past or the future instead of living in the present?

_____

_____

_____

_____

_____

_____

_____

_____

_____

_____

_____

_____

_____

"The present moment is the only time over which we have dominion."

THICH NHAT HANH

Take a moment to close your eyes and imagine a calm, safe place. This could be a place that you have in your life now, a place that you have been in the past, a place you hope to go one day, or a place that you can only imagine in your mind.

Draw or paint your relaxing place, remembering to set aside any self-judgment with the art. Notice how you feel as you work on your art and think about this place. Are you able to connect to the feeling of being calm and safe? Come back to this feeling any time you need to by visualizing this safe, peaceful place again.

People often try to be a version of themselves that reflects how they feel they should be or how others expect them to be. Think about an expectation from others or a way that you try to be that is not really true to who you are. For example, do you try to present yourself as someone who is cheerful and friendly, even when you don't feel like it? Write about why you've tried to be that person, and how it might change things if you chose to accept and share the true version of yourself.

---

*"I get so distracted by the way
I wish I were,
or the way I assume I am,
that I lose sight of
what's actually true."*

GRETCHEN RUBIN

Practice mindful movement while you take a walk or go for a run, preferably somewhere that you can feel connected to nature. Remind yourself to be present and aware. What do you notice both around you and within? What do you observe that is interesting, beautiful, or new to you? Try to engage all of your senses during this activity. Come back to this page and describe what you observed around you, what you noticed within, and how you felt.

_____

_____

_____

_____

_____

_____

_____

_____

_____

_____

_____

_____

_____

_____

"Looking at beauty in the world is the first step of purifying the mind."

AMIT RAY

A mandala is a circular drawing made up of repeating patterns. Although the word *mandala* comes from Sanskrit, this type of circular, geometric design is found in many cultures around the world. It's often connected with meditation practice.

One way to create a mandala is to first draw or trace a single circle or a set of concentric circles. Fill in your circle with repeating patterns and shapes. Add color if you wish. While you work on your mandala, try to practice an attitude of mindfulness—be present and, nonjudgmental, and set aside other worries or thoughts. Notice any unhelpful self-talk that comes up and try to reframe it.

Many people notice the negative things in their lives more easily than the positive ones. You can improve your mood by taking time to consciously notice the things that are good in your life. Think back on your past week and list as many good things as you can. You might think about what has gone well, examples of connection with others, things you have accomplished, or moments of enjoyment.

"Our life is shaped by our mind;

we become what we think."

BUDDHA

Check-in: Take some time to reflect on how you have been doing lately. What are some of the helpful things that you have done for your mental health? What has been stressful or challenging for you? Identify one example of how you have put into practice something you have explored through your journaling.

_____

_____

_____

_____

_____

_____

_____

_____

_____

_____

_____

_____

_____

Actively noticing and drawing on your strengths can help you to feel good about yourself and manage life's difficulties. Unfortunately, people tend to easily name all the ways in which they are not good enough, but struggle to identify their own strengths, especially if they experience depression and anxiety.

People also tend to downplay their own strengths because they assume "everyone is able to do that" or that their abilities are not a big deal. Take some time to identify and list your own strengths, like hope, kindness, determination, or humor. Then write about how these strengths have helped you through challenging situations and how you use them in your day-to-day life. (If you need some ideas, turn to page 158 for a list of strengths.)

_____

_____

_____

_____

_____

_____

_____

*"What I am is good enough
if I would only be it openly."*

CARL R. ROGERS

Create an image showcasing your strengths and values.
One option is to depict an example of you demonstrating just one of your strengths or values. Another option is to fill this page with symbols representing several of your strengths and values. Look back at your journaling about strengths on page 106 if you need inspiration.

Finding meaning, identifying positive outcomes, and recognizing your own growth are helpful responses to a negative experience or a difficult life event. This does not mean that you are glad that it happened, though it does help you see the negative experience in a more positive and productive way.

Write about a difficult experience that comes to mind, either a recent one or one from the past. It could be a setback in your career, the end of a relationship, managing a health problem, or something else in your life. Then write about how that experience helped you grow. Think about if it led to something more positive in your life, or how it fits into the purpose and meaning of your life.

_____

_____

_____

_____

_____

_____

_____

_____

_____

_____

"Nothing ever goes away until it has taught us what we need to know."

PEMA CHÖDRÖN

What would your ideal day look like? Take a moment to write about how you would spend your time, how you would feel, and who you would spend it with. What can you do to make more time in your life for these activities and the people who bring you joy and calm?

_____

_____

_____

_____

_____

_____

_____

_____

_____

_____

_____

_____

_____

_____

_____

*"When you recover or discover
something that nourishes your soul
and brings joy,
care enough about yourself
to make room for it in your life."*

JEAN SHINODA BOLEN

Create an image or collage about what brings you joy.
Think of a recent happy moment and represent it on the page. Another option is to fill this page with several images of people, places, and things that bring positivity into your life. You can choose to draw, paint, glue in collage images, or combine more than one for a mixed media approach.

Don't wait for someday; what is something you have been avoiding or putting off? It could be a big dream you've always wanted to achieve or a difficult task to complete. Write about what thoughts and obstacles get in the way.

How are anxiety, fear, or self-doubt showing up? Perhaps you are afraid of failing or doubt your ability to accomplish what is needed. Imagine how it will feel to accomplish this task or goal. Write down how you will take the steps toward completing this goal. What are some helpful thoughts that you want to remember?

_____

_____

_____

_____

_____

_____

_____

_____

_____

_____

"When you do a thing, do it with all your might. Put your whole soul into it. Stamp it with your personality. Be active, be energetic, be enthusiastic and faithful, and you will accomplish your object."

RALPH WALDO EMERSON

Practicing acceptance means acknowledging that you cannot change or control certain things. Instead of dwelling on the things you can't change, focus on changing your reaction to them. Write about a situation or relationship in your life in which you want to practice more acceptance. Look back at what you have written. If you notice sentences that include judgment or strong emotion, rewrite them with an attitude of neutral, nonjudgmental acceptance.

_____

_____

_____

_____

_____

_____

_____

_____

_____

_____

_____

_____

_____

_____

"Life is not the way it's supposed to be. It's the way it is. The way you cope with it is what makes the difference."

VIRGINIA SATIR

Check-in: How have you been able to draw on your strengths and coping skills to get through difficulties? Write about a recent challenge or stressor. What are the emotions and thoughts that came up? What coping skills and strengths were you able to use? Looking back, is there a strength or coping skill that you wish you had tried?

_____

_____

_____

_____

_____

_____

_____

_____

_____

_____

_____

_____

_____

_____

_____

_____

Blind contour drawing can help you practice mindfulness skills such as focus, observation, and nonjudgment. Grab a pencil or pen and then choose something nearby that you want to draw—a plant, a cup, your pet. Focusing on a single object works best for the first time you try this. Put your pencil on the page and look up at the object. Begin to draw, moving your eyes along the edge of the object as you move your hand on the page. Keep your pencil on the paper and do not look back down at your page until you are done. Remember that your drawing will probably not look very good; the goal is to practice observing and being present.

Placing negative labels on yourself—or believing the ones that you hear from others—damages your confidence and self-esteem. What is one negative label that you are ready to give up? What would you like to believe about yourself instead? Write about where this label came from for you and what it would change if you chose to stop believing it were true.

"Love yourself first and everything else falls into line. You really have to love yourself to get anything done in this world."

LUCILLE BALL

The voice you hear inside your head that speaks of doubt and self-judgment is called your inner critic. It's easy to get stuck in negative feelings triggered by your inner critic and act on its messages. But recognizing this voice can help you take away its power. When does your inner critic show up? Write about one or two situations that trigger your own inner critic and the messages it tells you.

Now, flip the script and think about your inner voice that offers guidance, encouragement, and kindness to yourself. I think of this voice as my inner guide, but you might want to use another name, like inner muse, cheerleader, sage, or coach. Give this part of yourself a name and then write down some of the messages it offers.

_____

_____

_____

_____

_____

_____

_____

_____

_____

_____

"All that you need is deep within you waiting to unfold and reveal itself. All you have to do is be still and take time to seek for what is within, and you will surely find it."

EILEEN CADDY

Understanding where your inner critic comes from can also help you understand it and respond when it is triggered. Think about the past experiences and messages from others that have shaped your inner critic. Consider that your inner critic is often speaking out of a place of fear and trying to protect you in some way. Write about how this part of yourself is actually trying to help. End your writing with a statement of gratitude toward your inner critic (e.g., "Thank you for trying to protect me from . . . ").

_____

_____

_____

_____

_____

_____

_____

_____

_____

_____

_____

_____

"Just because you've made mistakes doesn't mean your mistakes get to make you. Take notice of your inner critic, forgive yourself, and move on."

ROBERT TEW

Look back at your journaling on page 126 about your inner critic and inner guide (or whatever name you chose for your more supportive self-talk voice). Use art techniques— drawing, painting, or collage—to create an image of each one. These images can help you externalize the negative messages of the inner critic, and befriend and dialogue with these parts of yourself, allowing you to draw on the strength of your more supportive voice when needed.

Accomplishment often brings a boost in mood, but sometimes people minimize their accomplishments or focus too much on what has not yet been done. Start by thinking of all the things you have accomplished today—no matter how small. Now, turn your attention back to some of the other things you have done or achieved in the past weeks, months, and years. Fill these pages with writing about what you have accomplished. What is one of those accomplishments that you are especially proud of? Mark it in your writing with a star or by underlining it.

_____

_____

_____

_____

_____

_____

_____

_____

_____

_____

_____

_____

_____

*"If you want to be successful,
it's just this simple. Know what you
are doing. Love what you are doing.
And believe in what you are doing."*

WILL ROGERS

Check-in: You have made a lot of progress through this journal and it's time for another check-in. What has shifted in the way you think of yourself and your life? Write down an example of a new belief that you have. How does this new way of thinking impact your mood and your actions?

_____

_____

_____

_____

_____

_____

_____

_____

_____

_____

_____

_____

_____

_____

_____

Turning a scribble into an image is a way to tap into your creative intuition. Do a quick scribble on the page. Then spend some time looking at it and thinking about what your scribble could become. You might need to turn the page in a different direction. Add additional lines and color to develop your image. After you are done, give your art piece a title and consider what message it has for you.

For the next few minutes, write about the thoughts, stresses, and worries that have been on your mind. Then close your eyes and spend a few minutes meditating on letting these things pass. Think of an intention, short phrase, or word that you want to focus on instead of what is distressing you. As you breathe out, imagine letting go of what is bothering you. As you breathe in, feel yourself relax. Repeat your intention or relaxation word to yourself with each breath.

_____

_____

_____

_____

_____

_____

_____

_____

_____

_____

*"That's life: starting over,
one breath at a time."*

SHARON SALZBERG

How do you feel about asking for help; is it easy or difficult?
Write about your beliefs around asking for help. Is there a specific experience that has shaped your point of view? If asking for help has been difficult for you in the past, what is a new belief or thought that you would like to have about vulnerability and asking for help?

Write down at least one way you will reach out to someone for help and support soon and, then come back to this page later and write about how you felt and how it went. If asking for help is usually easy for you, write about a time that getting help from someone was especially meaningful and important for you.

"All of us, at some time or other, need help. Whether we're giving or receiving help, each one of us has something valuable to bring to this world. That's one of the things that connects us as neighbors—in our own way, each one of us is a giver and a receiver."

FRED ROGERS

In the center of the page, draw an image that represents a current problem. This could be a challenging relationship, career difficulties, or a mental health struggle. You can choose to draw a representational picture that depicts the situation or something that is more symbolic or abstract. Around your image of the problem, add symbols, colors, and words to represent possible solutions. Your solutions could include inner strengths, coping skills, support from others, or helpful actions. Do you notice any shift in your thoughts or feelings about the problem after completing your artwork?

It's important to be able to recognize your personal warning signs. These are certain physical or emotional signs that let you know your life is out of balance or your mental health may be suffering. For example, you might notice back pain or getting sick, snapping at your family members more often, or increasing your alcohol intake.

Noticing them is a signal to yourself that it is time to make a change, recommit to your self-care, or ask for help. Make a list of your own warning signs—emotions, thinking patterns, physical symptoms, and behaviors—that let you know it's time to pay more attention to your mental health.

_____

_____

_____

_____

_____

_____

_____

_____

_____

_____

_____

"Our greatest weakness lies in giving up. The most certain way to succeed is always to try just one more time."

THOMAS EDISON

Imagine that you are at the end of your life, looking back. Assuming you've lived your best life, what do you see? What have you done and who was in your life? Maybe you see family and friends, a certain career or accomplishment, places you have traveled, and the small joys of daily life. What aspects of your life have been the most important to you and what values have you lived by?

_____

_____

_____

_____

_____

_____

_____

_____

_____

_____

_____

_____

"Your time is limited, so don't waste it living someone else's life.
Don't be trapped by dogma—which is living with the results of other people's thinking. Don't let the noise of others' opinions drown out your own inner voice. And most important, have the courage to follow your heart and intuition."

STEVE JOBS

Think of an intention, mantra, or helpful phrase that you want to focus on in your life right now. Write your word or phrase on this page and incorporate it into a piece of art by adding color, doodles, images, or collage. Return to this page whenever you need some inspiration.

Check-in: Let's take some time to reflect on both your progress and what you need to keep working on. How has your mental health shifted during this experience and what changes have been most helpful? What are three things you will commit to continue doing to keep yourself present and grounded?

_____

_____

_____

_____

_____

_____

_____

_____

_____

_____

_____

_____

_____

Final Reflection

As you come to the end of this journal, I hope you feel good about all the work you have done to care for yourself. Remember that good mental health is an ongoing process, requiring continued work and maintenance. Many of the things addressed in this book should be incorporated into your life on a continuous basis—listening to your emotions and needs, cultivating supportive relationships, making time for movement, practicing mindfulness, and using healthy coping skills. Making these things a part of your life helps keep you on the path of good mental health.

Continuing to journal and being creative may also help your mental health. You can revisit some of these writing prompts again to guide future journaling. Repeating an exercise can help you reinforce a new skill or mind-set. You may also find that some of these prompts can help you sort through thoughts, feelings, and challenges that come up around future concerns. Many of the creative prompts can also be repeated for future stress reduction and enjoyment.

When you notice that things seem out of balance or you get overwhelmed by the stresses of life, remember that there are things you can do to help yourself. Give yourself time to reflect on your feelings and needs and then take action to improve your mood. You deserve to live a life of happiness and fulfillment.

Identify Your Feelings

Happy	Serene	Courageous
Joyful	Content	Determined
Cheerful	Peaceful	Capable
Glad	Comfortable	Sensitive
Delighted	Loving	Sad
Excited	Amiable	Awful
Grateful	Compassionate	Depressed
Elated	Empathic	Lonely
Inspired	Nurturing	Gloomy
Proud	Receptive	Hopeless
Satisfied	Thoughtful	Discouraged
Terrific	Generous	Hurt
Thrilled	Appreciated	Miserable
Amused	Strong	Abandoned
Playful	Bold	Rejected
Hopeful	Adventurous	Melancholic
Surprised	Confident	Empty
Agreeable	Powerful	Grief-stricken
Pensive	Motivated	Disappointed
Stable	Fearless	Tired
Calm	Energetic	Exhausted
Relaxed	Daring	Insecure

Uncertain	Worried	Disagreeable
Vulnerable	Hesitant	Grumpy
Shaken	Tense	Frustrated
Helpless	Uneasy	Mad
Fragile	Afraid	Irritated
Numb	Scared	Furious
Bored	Frightened	Rageful
Dissociated	Terrified	Bitter
Ambivalent	Alarmed	Combative
Ashamed	Panicked	Defiant
Embarrassed	Overwhelmed	Jealous
Inadequate	Restless	Envious
Humiliated	Distracted	Hateful
Ignored	Agitated	Selfish
Neglected	Confused	Impatient
Disconnected	Reluctant	Outraged
Invalidated	Awkward	Rebellious
Distressed	Exasperated	Unfriendly
Shy	Angry	Vindictive
Anxious	Upset	
Nervous	Annoyed	

Self-Care Ideas

Listen to music.

Spend time outdoors.

Get some exercise.

Do meditation, yoga, or a mindfulness practice.

Take slow, deep breaths for a few minutes.

Garden or care for plants.

Eat healthy foods throughout the day.

Drink plenty of water.

Eat a special treat.

Limit your caffeine and alcohol intake.

Get enough sleep every night.

Take a nap.

Make time for enjoyable and fun activities.

Journal.

Spend time with friends who are fun and supportive.

Create, do art, craft, or build something.

Read for pleasure, not just school or work.

Listen to a podcast or audiobook.

Get organized and clean your home.

Tackle a task you have been avoiding.

Explore new places or try new activities.

Spend time with pets.

Pray, attend church, or participate in other spiritual activities.

Laugh.

Listen to and accept your feelings.

Express gratitude to yourself or others.

Wake up at a consistent time each day.

Take medications as prescribed.

Get help for or take care of illness and injury.

Refocus on something else instead of ruminating.

Inspire yourself with poems, quotes, or images.

Wear clothes that express yourself, make you feel good, or are comfortable.

Make time for personal hygiene or grooming tasks.

Get a massage.

Say no when you need to.

Ask for help.

Balance responsibilities and fun.

Find Your Strengths

Adaptability

Adventurousness

Ambition

Analytical Thinking

Assertiveness

Athleticism

Attention to Detail

Authenticity

Balance

Belief

Bravery

Calm

Capability

Care for Others

Caution

Charisma

Cheerfulness

Citizenship

Commitment

Communication

Compassion

Competitiveness

Confidence

Connecting to Others

Conscientiousness

Consideration

Courage

Creativity

Critical Thinking

Curiosity

Decisiveness

Dedication

Deliberation

Dependability

Diligence

Discipline

Emotional Intelligence

Empathy

Energy

Enthusiasm

Equity

Fairness

Faith

Flexibility

Focus	Inventiveness
Forgiveness	Judgment
Friendliness	Justice
Fun-Loving	Kindness
Generosity	Knowledge
Gentleness	Leadership
Gratitude	Learning
Growth Mind-set	Logic
Hard Work	Love
Helpfulness	Loyalty
Honesty	Meticulousness
Hope	Modesty
Humility	Motivation
Humor	Nurturing
Idealism	Observant
Imagination	Open-Mindedness
Inclusiveness	Optimism
Independence	Organization
Industriousness	Originality
Insight	Passion
Integrity	Patience
Intuition	Peacefulness

Persistence

Perspective

Persuasiveness

Playfulness

Positivity

Problem-Solving

Prudence

Punctuality

Resilience

Resourcefulness

Respect

Responsibility

Seeing the Big Picture

Self-Awareness

Self-Control

Selfless

Sense of Purpose

Social Intelligence

Spirituality

Spontaneity

Strategic Thinking

Strength

Teamwork

Thoroughness

Thrift

Trustworthiness

Understanding

Wisdom

Resources

Cohen, Barry M., Mary-Michola Barnes, and Anita B. Rankin. *Managing Traumatic Stress Through Art: Drawing from the Center.* Baltimore: The Sidran Press, 1995.

Greenberger, Dennis and Christine A. Padesky. *Mind Over Mood: Change How You Feel by Changing the Way You Think.* New York: The Guilford Press, 1995.

Harris, Dan. *Ten Percent Happier* Podcast. https://www.tenpercent.com/podcast.

McKay, Matthew, Jeffrey C. Wood, and Jeffrey Brantley. *The Dialectical Behavior Therapy Skills Workbook: Practical DBT Exercises for Learning Mindfulness, Interpersonal Effectiveness, Emotion Regulation, and Distress Tolerance.* Oakland: New Harbinger Publications, Inc., 2007.

Neff, Kristin. *Self-Compassion.* https://self-compassion.org.

Acknowledgments

Thank you to my husband and son, who supported me throughout this project, giving me encouragement and the extra time to get the writing done. My husband has told me for many years now that I would write a book one day, believing it before I ever did. My son is my biggest motivation to keep myself present and grounded. Thank you to my parents who have always believed that I can do anything that I decide to do, sharing their love and pride throughout the years. And gratitude to all the educators, supervisors, and fellow therapists that have helped me learn and implement the ideas that are included in this journal.

About the Author

 **Carolyn Mehlomakulu, LMFT-S, ATR-BC,** is a psychotherapist and art therapist in Austin, Texas. In her private practice (TherapyWithCarolyn.com), she works with individuals and families of all ages to help them overcome depression, anxiety, and trauma. Carolyn also facilitates art therapy groups for teens and adults in an outpatient clinic. Her past experience includes working in residential foster care, probation services, school-based therapy, and community mental health. Through her blog Creativity in Therapy (CreativityInTherapy.com), Carolyn supports counselors and therapists in using art therapy and other creative therapeutic approaches by offering articles, resources, workshops, and online training. Carolyn graduated from Loyola Marymount University with a master's degree in marital and family therapy, with specialized training in art therapy.

CPSIA information can be obtained
at www.ICGtesting.com
Printed in the USA
JSHW022014150420
5096JS00001B/1